Usborne Early Years
Wipe-clean
Starting to Write

Illustrated by Genine Delahaye

Written by

Jessica Greenwell

Designed by

Stephanie Jeffries

Write your name here, if you want to.

Romena

Trace over all the round shapes and wavy lines under the sea.

Always start at the big dot.

Trace over the loops on my shell.

These letters are made using round shapes. Trace over them and write some more.

Trace over all the long and straight lines in this picture.

Trace over the long lines on my ladder.

Start at the big dot.

These letters are made using long lines. Trace over them and write some more.

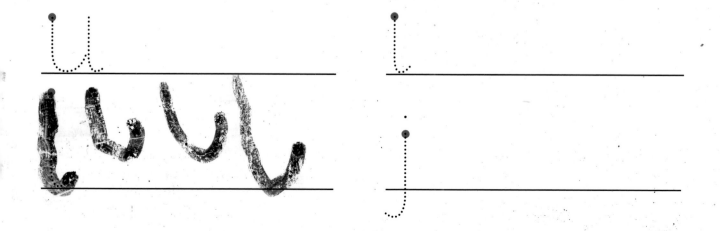

Trace over the
pattern on the roof
to practise the shapes
for 'u' and 'y'.

Trace over all the zigzag lines in this snowy scene.

Start at the big dot.

Trace over the snowy mountain peaks.

Weeee!

These letters are made using zigzag lines. Trace over them and write some more.

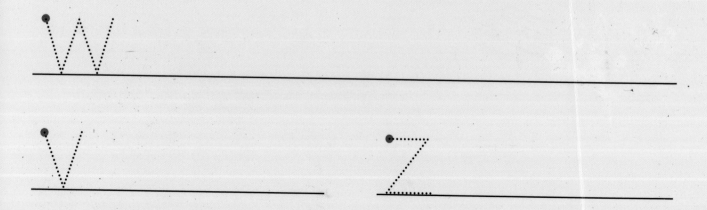

Trace over the animals' letters and say each letter sound.

'b' for bear!

What sound does my letter make?

Start at the big dot.

b   c   r

Which of their letters should start the first word below?
Copy it into the space. Then, find letters for the other words.

_____ all

_____ obot

BEEP BEEP

_____ up

Did you find them?

Which word below begins with 'p'? Write it in the space.

d

p

k

What does it begin with?

___ ite

___ uck

___ en

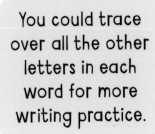

You could trace over all the other letters in each word for more writing practice.

Trace over these animals' letters and say each letter sound.

'a' is for alligator.

Start at the big dot.

Which of their letters should start the first word below?
Copy it into the space. Then, find letters for the other words.

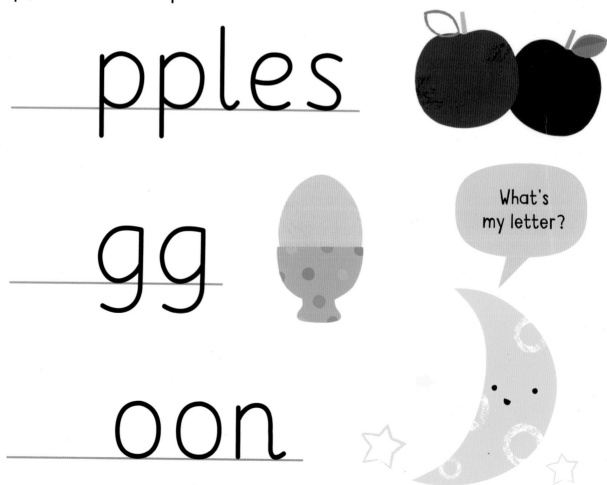

pples

gg

What's my letter?

oon

Trace over the three-letter words at the beach. Then, copy them onto the lines.

sun
sun

The first one has been done for you.

sea

Aaargh!

hat

wet

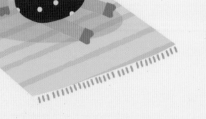

Which word below begins with my letter? Copy the letter into the space.

___ish

___urtle

___eaf

hut

bag

rod

net

be

Trace over and copy the dotted words in this picture.

Start at the big dot each time.

bus

_____

cap

_____

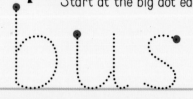

My cap!

_____

hug

_____

jog

_____

car

van

box

fox

It's Sport's Day!
Trace over and
copy all of these
doing words.

hop

skip

jump

run

hit

win

Catch!

THWACK

You won
the cup!

Hooray!

1st

2nd

3rd

clap
clap

Choose from the letters on the sign to complete each word below. Copy the correct letter into each gap. The first one has been done for you.

t_nt

p_n

h_t

These animal words have been muddled up. Unscramble them and copy the correct letters into each box.

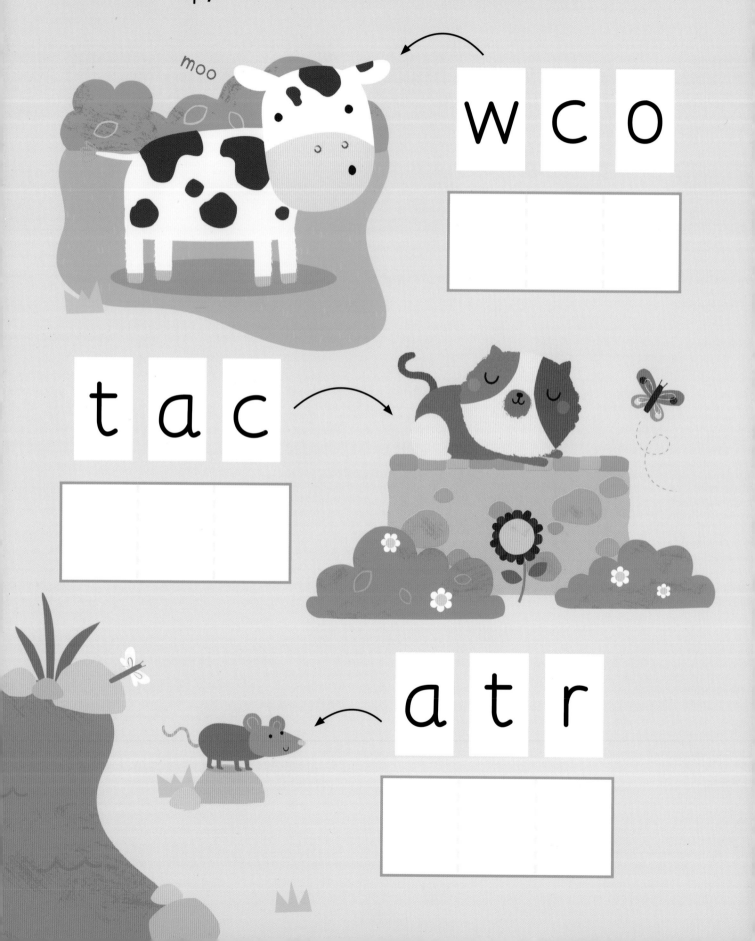

moo

w c o

t a c

a t r

cluck

e h n

g i p

oink

bzzz

g d o

Copy the missing words into the gaps in these sentences.

cat

car

The _____ is in a _____.

fox

ship

A _____ is on the _____.